GO FACTS PLANTS

Flowers

FALKIRK COUNCIL
LIBRARY SUPPORT
FOR SCHOOLS

A & C BLACK · LONDON

Flowers

contents

© Blake Publishing Pty Ltd 2002
Additional Material © A & C Black Publishers Ltd 2003

First published 2002 in Australia by Blake Education Pty Ltd

This edition published 2003 in the United Kingdom by
A&C Black Publishers Ltd, 37 Soho Square, London W1D 3QZ
www.acblack.com

Published by permission of Blake Publishing Pty Ltd, Glebe NSW, Australia.
All rights reserved. No part of this publication may be reproduced in any
form or by any means – graphic, electronic or mechanical, including
photocopying, recording, taping or information storage and retrieval systems
– without the prior written permission of the publishers.

ISBN 0-7136-6607-2

A CIP record for this book is available from the British Library.

Written by Paul McEvoy
Science Consultant: Dr Will Edwards, School of Tropical Biology,
James Cook University
Design and layout by The Modern Art Production Group
Photos by Photodisc, Stockbyte, John Foxx, Corbis, Imagin,
Artville and Corel

UK Series Consultant: Julie Garnett

Printed in Hong Kong by Wing King Tong Co Ltd

A & C Black uses paper produced with elemental chlorine-free pulp,
harvested from managed sustainable forests.

Flowering Plants

Flowering plants all grow flowers which make seeds. They are the largest group of plants.

Many plants in our gardens and parks grow large, colourful flowers. Other plants, like grasses, have small flowers that are hard to see.

rose

Flowers are how most plants grow new seeds. Grasses, shrubs and vines all grow flowers. Most trees, except for conifers, also grow flowers. Even cacti and waterlilies grow flowers.

Flowers attract insects and birds with their bright colours. These animals feed on the **nectar** inside the flowers.

4

Waterlilies grow in lakes and ponds.

rhododendron

Wisteria is a flowering vine.

GO FACTS

TALLEST!

The mountain ash tree is the tallest flowering plant in the world. It can grow as high as 92 metres.

What is a Flower?

Flowers make seeds. Seeds grow into new plants. Each part of a flower has a purpose.

The petals of a flower are what we notice first. Petals can be colourful and might smell sweet. Their bright colours attract insects and birds.

At the heart of the flower are egg cells called **ovules**. They are found at the base of the flower in the **ovary**. Out of the ovary grows a stalk-like style. At the end of the **style** is the **stigma**. The stigma is sticky so that **pollen** from other flowers will cling to it.

poppies

A circle of **stamens** grows around the stigma. Each stamen holds a pollen sac called an **anther**. Anthers produce thousands of tiny pollen grains. Pollen is often yellow. Insects, birds and the wind move pollen from flower to flower.

A flower has petals, a stigma and stamens.
Each part of a flower is important.

The Parts of a Flower

Can you see the different parts of each flower?

See if you can find these flower parts:
- the petals
- the style in the middle of the flower
- the sticky stigma
- the circle of stamens
- the pollen sacs called anthers.

How do you think the pollen from another flower gets to the ovule?

lilium

poppy

8

lily

pelargonium

passionflower

hibiscus

passionflower

9

From Flower to Fruit

Seeds and fruit grow from flowers. Each flower must be pollinated before it can make fruit and seeds.

1 A flower begins as a tight bud. These are the buds of apple tree flowers.

2 The apple blossom opens. Bees or other insects carry pollen from one flower to another. This is called **pollination**. After pollination a grain of pollen combines with each ovule. Each pollinated ovule may become a seed.

3 The petals drop off the flower and the apple grows.

4 Inside each apple are the seeds for a new plant.

Types of Flowers

Flowers come in many sizes, colours and shapes. They vary from tiny grass flowers to the giant flowers of the tropics.

Regular flowers have petals that are all shaped the same. The buttercup and the wild rose are regular flowers. Irregular flowers have petals that are different shapes. Snapdragons and orchids are irregular flowers.

The large centres of daisies and sunflowers are made up of many tiny flowers. Each one can make a seed.

buttercups

sunflower

Orchids are the most **complex** of all flowers. They attract insects and often have a lip where insects can land. The insect's head gets brushed with pollen as it drinks nectar.

orchid

wheat flowers

Grasses are flowering plants. Wheat, rice and corn are all grasses. They have very small flowers that are hard to see. The wind pollinates these flowers.

Do Flowers Drink Water?

If the petals change colour, you can see that flowers really do drink water.

You will need:

- white flowers—carnations work well
- food colouring
- a tall glass
- water

Directions:

1 Place some food colouring and water in the glass.

2 Cut the stem of the flower.

3 Place the flower in the glass. Leave for a few hours.

Now try this.

Split the stem down the middle and place each half in different-coloured water.

blue colouring

red and blue colouring

red colouring

yellow colouring

Flowers Need Animals

Many animals feed on the nectar from flowers. As a result the animals carry pollen from flower to flower.

Many insects feed on flowers. Flowers have colour and perfume to attract insects. As insects feed on the nectar, they also pick up some pollen. The pollen catches a ride to the next flower. After being pollinated, flowers make seeds.

Birds, bats and even some lizards are also attracted to flowers. These animals like flowers with plenty of nectar. The flowers feed the animals, and the animals carry pollen to the next flower.

Hummingbirds feed on nectar.

A swallowtail butterfly feeding on a flower.

Bees collect nectar and pollen.

GO FACTS

DID YOU KNOW?
About 2 000 types of birds feed on nectar from flowers.

The Seeds of Life

The area under a plant may not get enough sunlight for seeds to grow into healthy plants. Seeds are carried away by wind, water and animals so that the plants grow in new places.

Many seeds have parts that catch the wind. Dandelion seeds are like tiny parachutes. The wind picks them up and carries them away. Sycamore seeds are more like helicopters that twirl in the wind.

Some seeds float. Rain, rivers or even the sea can carry these seeds to a new home. Coconuts can travel a long way before they start life on a new beach.

coconut

Some seeds are wrapped in tasty fruits, and animals carry them away. Mammals or birds eat the fruit and spit out the seeds. Even if an animal eats the seeds, they can still grow out of the animal's droppings.

White clematis seeds have fluffy heads to catch the wind.

Monkeys travel through the forest looking for ripe fruit.

dandelion

Dandelion seeds catch the wind.

GO FACTS

MOST!

The seed capsule of an orchid can hold up to 20 000 seeds.

19

Habitats

Flowering plants are able to live in many different parts of the world. Rainforests, deserts and cold mountains are all homes to different flowering plants.

Rainforests get plenty of what plants need — rain, warmth and sunshine — so plants grow in great numbers. A huge variety of flowering plants, such as trees, vines and other **tropical** plants, grow in rainforests.

Deserts are hot, dry places and water is in short supply. Plants need to be able to store water and wait for rain. Cactus plants have thick, fleshy stems that hold water and sharp spines to protect them from animals.

Some places, such as **alpine** areas, have very long, cold winters, short summers and strong winds. Plants cannot grow in frozen ground. Short summers mean that plants need to grow, flower and make seeds quickly. Where there are strong winds, plants don't grow very tall.

Cacti flower in the desert.

Heliconias grow in rainforests.

Alpine flowers cover whole mountain sides in spring and summer.

Does it Flower?

Yes

No

22

Glossary

alpine	high mountain areas where no trees grow
anther	the part of the stamen that produces the pollen
complex	having many parts
nectar	the sweet juice of flowers
ovary	where the ovules are stored
ovule	egg cells in flowers
pollen	the powder on a flower's stamens
pollination	the movement of pollen from stamen to stigma
stamen	the pollen-bearing part of a flower
stigma	the flower part that pollen sticks to
style	the flower part that supports the stigma
tropics	areas of land near the Equator

Index

FALKIRK COUNCIL
LIBRARY SUPPORT
FOR SCHOOLS